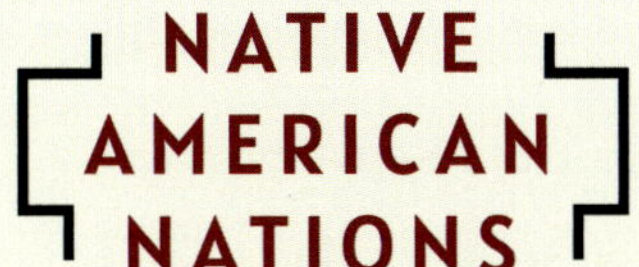

Shoshone

F.A. BIRD

Checkerboard Library

An Imprint of Abdo Publishing
abdobooks.com

ABDOBOOKS.COM
Published by Abdo Publishing, a division of ABDO, PO Box 398166, Minneapolis, Minnesota 55439.

Printed in the United States of America, North Mankato, Minnesota
102024
012025

Editor: Lauri Nelson
Design: Mighty Media, Inc.

Cover Photograph: Danita Delimont Photography/Newscom
Interior Photographs: Ad_hominem/Shutterstock Images, p. 7; Alpha Stock/Alamy Stock Photo, p. 13; Angel Wynn/NativeStock, pp. 23, 29; B Brown/Shutterstock Images, p. 11; Ben Wittick/Buyenlarge/Getty Images, p. 9; Bettmann/Getty Images, p. 25; CORBIS/Corbis via Getty Images, p. 17; Idaho State Historical Society/Prospector Club Archives, p. 21; Otto Herschan Collection/Hulton Archive/Getty Images, p. 19; Tucker James/Shutterstock Images, p. 5; Werner Forman/Universal Images Group/Getty Images, p. 15; Zack Frank/Shutterstock Images, p. 27

Library of Congress Control Number: 2024938814

Publisher's Cataloging-in-Publication Data
Names: Bird, F.A., author.
Title: Shoshone / by F.A. Bird
Description: Minneapolis, Minnesota : ABDO Publishing, 2025 | Series: Native American nations | Includes online resources and index.
Identifiers: ISBN 9781098296261 (lib. bdg.) | ISBN 9798384917373 (ebook)
Subjects: LCSH: Shoshoni Indians--Juvenile literature. | Shoshone Indians--Juvenile literature. | Native Americans--Juvenile literature. | Indians of North America--Juvenile literature. | Indigenous peoples--Social life and customs--Juvenile literature. | Cultural anthropology--Juvenile literature.
Classification: DDC 973.0497--dc23

Contents

Homelands ... 4
Society ... 6
Homes ... 8
Food ... 10
Clothing ... 12
Crafts ... 14
Family ... 16
Children ... 18
Traditions ... 20
War ... 22
Contact with Europeans ... 24
Washakie ... 26
The Shoshone Today ... 28
Glossary ... 30
Online Resources ... 31
Index ... 32

Homelands

The Shoshone (shuh-SHO-nee) call themselves *Newe* or *Nimi*. This name means "the people" in their language. Shoshone homelands once included parts of present-day Wyoming, Montana, Utah, Idaho, California, and Nevada.

The Shoshone lived west of the Bighorn Mountains and east of the Snake River. Their territory stretched northward to present-day Montana. To the south, Shoshone territory reached the Uinta Mountains and the Green River. Some western Shoshone territory reached present-day southeastern California.

Shoshone homelands contained plains, basins, canyons, valleys, and mountains. There were also lakes, streams, ponds, marshes, rivers, and even deserts. These areas were home to many types of fish, birds, and animals. Trees, shrubs, berries, wildflowers, and other plants grew on the land.

Blackfoot River near Wolverine Canyon in Idaho

Society

The Shoshone lived in bands made up of extended families. Each band was named after its leader or after a river near the band's settlement.

Shoshone bands were **seminomadic**. They followed the **migrating** animals and the ripening of wild plants. They made seasonal rounds to gather, hunt, and fish.

Each band had a leader. The leader, or chief, led by the agreement of everyone and not by force. Shoshone society had other leaders, too. A war leader made sure that the people were protected from enemies. Spiritual leaders' lives centered on religion.

The Shoshone also had medicine people who interpreted dreams and aided in **vision quests**. They offered thanks to the Creator for plants and animals, which the Shoshone needed to survive. Medicine people also healed with **rituals** and herbs. And, they conducted annual ceremonies.

THE SHOSHONE HOMELANDS
BRITISH COLUMBIA
ALBERTA
SASKATCHEWAN
MANITOBA
ONTARIO
QUEBEC
PRINCE EDWARD ISLAND
NEW BRUNSWICK
NOVA SCOTIA
Lake Superior
Lake Michigan
Lake Huron
Lake Ontario
Lake Erie
Ottawa River
St. Lawrence River
WASHINGTON
OREGON
CALIFORNIA
NEVADA
IDAHO
MONTANA
WYOMING
UTAH
ARIZONA
COLORADO
NEW MEXICO
NORTH DAKOTA
SOUTH DAKOTA
NEBRASKA
KANSAS
OKLAHOMA
TEXAS
MINNESOTA
IOWA
MISSOURI
ARKANSAS
LOUISIANA
WISCONSIN
ILLINOIS
MICHIGAN
INDIANA
OHIO
KENTUCKY
TENNESSEE
MISSISSIPPI
ALABAMA
GEORGIA
FLORIDA
SOUTH CAROLINA
NORTH CAROLINA
VIRGINIA
WEST VIRGINIA
PENNSYLVANIA
NEW YORK
MAINE
VERMONT
NEW HAMPSHIRE
MASSACHUSETTS
RHODE ISLAND
CONNECTICUT
NEW JERSEY
DELAWARE
MARYLAND
WASHINGTON, DC
ALASKA
HAWAII
N
W
E
S
THE SHOSHONE HOMELANDS

Homes

The Shoshone lived in different kinds of homes. During seasonal travel, the Shoshone often slept in brush shelters. These could be left behind as the people moved to other areas. They also made temporary shelters by stretching animal hides over a few poles to make a lean-to. Sometimes, the Shoshone even slept in caves.

During the winter, the Shoshone lived in cone-shaped tepees. They formed a tepee frame with sapling poles. They tied the poles at the top with cord or **rawhide**. Then they covered the frame with slabs of bark, grass, or animal hides. A hole in the top of the tepee let out smoke.

Sometimes, people piled stones along the outside of the tepee to anchor it and to block the wind. Inside, the people slept on fur robes and woven willow mats.

The Shoshone also made sweat houses. These buildings had wooden frames covered with earth and grass. Inside, men took sweat baths to cleanse their minds and bodies.

A tepee door was a flap of hide that could be in many positions to keep the people inside comfortable.

Food

The Shoshone hunted, fished, and gathered their food. The men caught small animals in snares and traps. They used bows and arrows, lances, and knives to hunt larger animals. These animals included elk, pronghorn, bighorn sheep, deer, and bison.

Men also fished for salmon, trout, and other fish. They used hook and line, nets, and spears to catch the fish. Men also caught fish by building a weir, a trap in the water. Fish swam into the weir and were easily caught.

Shoshone women also collected food for the family. They gathered wild vegetables, fruits, seeds, piñon nuts, berries, and **camas** roots. The women roasted the camas roots in a fire pit. They ground the cooked roots, and then made flour for bread, biscuits, and other treats.

The Shoshone were thankful for their food. They performed first ceremonies to give thanks to the plants, fish, and animals they depended on for survival.

A Shoshone fish trap catches salmon as they swim upstream.

Clothing

The Shoshone made clothing from bison, deer, pronghorn, and elk hides. They decorated their clothing with floral designs. To do this, they used materials such as porcupine quills, bones, hooves, and **ermine** tails. Later, the Shoshone began trading for glass seed beads. Then the women began using a combination of quills and beads.

Shoshone women wore fringed dresses. They decorated each dress with shells, horns, and elk teeth. Women also wore short leggings.

Men wore shirts that hung down to their thighs. They wore **breechcloths** and leggings. The leggings protected their legs from brush and thorns.

Shoshone men also wore headdresses. Traditionally, a man earned one eagle feather for each brave deed. So, a large eagle feather headdress meant a man was courageous and respected.

Traditional Shoshone clothing can be made with colorful fabrics today.

Crafts

Shoshone women created beautiful porcupine quillwork. They used quillwork to decorate shirts, dresses, leggings, armbands, bags, moccasins, and other clothing. Women often gathered in quillwork circles for this. They shared stories and taught the younger women how to quill.

To begin a quillwork project, women pulled quills from a porcupine hide. They cleaned the quills and sorted them according to size. Then, they dyed the quills. Dyes were made from wild onion skins, wild berries, and plant roots.

Quills were hard when dry. So, a woman would put a quill in her mouth to soften it. Then she would bite down on the quill to flatten it. Then, the quills were ready to use.

Next, women would sew the quills onto clothing. They used bone needles and **awls**, as well as thread made from bison **sinew**. A Shoshone woman often wore an awl around her neck. The awl's case was made out of heavy leather and decorated with quillwork.

A quillwork strip decorates a buffalo hide painting of a successful hunt.

CHAPTER 7
Family

Every family member was expected to contribute to the survival of the Shoshone band. Men, women, children, and elders all had their own responsibilities.

Men made tools for hunting and fishing. They carved bows from juniper wood, and then rubbed each bow with **tallow**. Next, they wrapped thin strips of **sinew** around the bow. This strengthened the bow and also made it waterproof. The Shoshone made the bowstring out of hemp fibers.

The women skillfully prepared fish and hides. They used scrapers to cut away the meat and hair from the hides. They **tanned** the leather with the animal's brains. Tanning softened the leather and prepared it for making clothing.

The Shoshone elders had responsibilities, too. They made horns and hooves into glue. The Shoshone also made bison horns into tools, cups, and bowls.

After women scraped an animal hide, they pegged it flat to the ground.

Children

The Shoshone loved and cared for their children. Parents carried their babies on willow **cradleboards**. Cradleboards kept babies safe and happy.

Older Shoshone children helped with daily chores, such as gathering wild berries, seeds, or vegetables. The children also helped gather pine nuts.

Shoshone children also learned from their elders. Elders taught children ceremonial songs and dances. They told children the stories of their people. Elders also taught children how to make four-holed flutes, bone whistles, and musical bows.

Shoshone children also had time to run, swim, and play. They played with whip tops. A whip top was about three inches (8 cm) tall and was carved from bone, wood, or stone. The children used leather thongs tied to one end of a long stick to whip the top. Each player tried to keep his or her top twirling longer than the other players' tops.

A Shoshone woman carries her child in a cradleboard.

Traditions

Native American nations often have stories that tell how people came to this world. One Shoshone version says that a long time ago Wolf created humans. Wolf placed them inside a willow jug basket. This jug basket was woven so tightly that it could hold water.

Wolf gave his brother Coyote a simple job. Wolf said, "Do not open the jug until you get to the Great Basin." Coyote said, "I can do that." Then he began on his journey.

When Coyote was on the east coast of North America, he heard drumming and singing. It was coming from inside the jug. Coyote, being curious, opened the jug. As soon as the jug opened, the humans ran out. They ran all over North and South America.

By the time Coyote got the jug closed, only a pair of humans remained inside. Coyote finally reached his destination. He opened the jug and out fell the pair. They became known as the Shoshone.

The Shoshone have many stories that use Coyote as a way to teach lessons.

War

Before the Shoshone had contact with Europeans, war rarely happened. Fights only occurred when hostile tribes entered Shoshone lands. When the Shoshone did need to fight, they were prepared with many different weapons.

Weapons of war were the same as hunting weapons for the Shoshone. They fought with bows and arrows, knives, and lances. They used an elk horn to sharpen knives and arrowhead points.

The warriors also used a club for fighting at close range. This weapon had a long handle covered with leather. Attached to the handle was a two-pound (1 kg) rock also covered in leather. When a warrior swung the club, the rock hit the target hard.

The Shoshone wore bone breastplates and chokers for protection. It was hard for an arrow, knife, or lance to pierce these bone plates. Warriors also made **rawhide** shields. They used bison rawhide because it was strong.

A Shoshone bone hairpipe breastplate was used for decoration as well as protection.

CHAPTER II

Contact with Europeans

Through trade with Europeans, the Shoshone obtained horses. Horses made hunting large animals, such as bison, much easier. However, neighboring tribes had also traded with the French for guns. Not having guns put the Shoshone at a disadvantage. Attacking tribes forced some Shoshone off their traditional lands.

In 1805, the Shoshone met a group of American explorers. The Lewis and Clark Expedition met the Lemhi band of Shoshone. The expedition was looking for a route to the Pacific Ocean. Sacagawea, a Shoshone woman, helped guide the men.

Over time, white settlers flooded into Shoshone territory. In 1863, about 200 Shoshone were killed along the Bear River by volunteer soldiers. Many Shoshone also died from diseases such as smallpox.

Sacagawea guides Lewis and Clark through the Rocky Mountains.

Washakie

Washakie (wahsh'-uh-kee) was a respected Shoshone leader, orator, and peacekeeper. The name *Washakie* means "**Rawhide** Rattle." Washakie received his name after making a rawhide rattle from the first bison he killed. He shook the rattle to scare the horses of his enemies.

In 1850, Washakie was principal chief of the Eastern Shoshone. He wanted to protect his people and maintain peace. He believed negotiating with the United States, rather than fighting, was the best way.

Washakie worked as a scout for General George Cook of the US Army. In 1868, Washakie negotiated a peace treaty that created the Wind River Reservation. He helped the settlers have safe passage.

In later years, Washakie grew unhappy with the United States. The Shoshone had been promised supplies, seeds, animals, and tools. But the US government did not uphold these treaty promises. Washakie died in 1900.

A statue of Washakie stands outside the Wyoming State Capitol Building.

The Shoshone Today

Today, there are more than 10,000 Shoshone tribal members. They have 14 **federally recognized** Shoshone reservations. These reservations are located in Utah, California, Wyoming, Idaho, and Nevada.

Shoshone elders are working hard to restore their language. College courses, dictionaries, and language apps teach the younger generations. The Shoshone do not want their language to disappear.

The Shoshone share their culture in many ways. Museums and cultural centers offer people ways to learn about the history, traditions, and current lives of the Shoshone. They have powwows to honor Shoshone culture through storytelling, music and dancing, arts, and food. There are traditional ceremonies such as the sun dance, bear dance, and round dance. These ceremonies include offering thanks.

Dancers gather for the Grand Entry at the Shoshone-Bannock Indian Festival in Idaho.

Glossary

awl—a pointed tool for marking or making small holes in materials, such as leather or wood.

breechcloth—a piece of hide or cloth, usually worn by men, that is wrapped between the legs and tied with a belt around the waist.

camas—an eatable plant found mostly in the western U.S.

cradleboard—a flat board used to hold a baby.

ermine—a weasel with a white coat.

federal recognition—the US government's recognition of a tribe as being an independent nation. The tribe is eligible for special funding and protection of its lands.

migrate—to move from one place to another.

rawhide—untanned cattle hide.

ritual—a form or order to a ceremony.

seminomad—a member of a people that moves from place to place, but has a home base where homes are built and crops are grown.

sinew—a band of tough fibers that joins a muscle to a bone.

tallow—the melted fat of cattle and sheep.

tan—to make a hide into leather by soaking it in a special liquid.

vision quest—a way for Native Americans to communicate with nature and the spirit world. People on vision quests seek advice, answers to questions, and an understanding of why they have come to the earth.

ONLINE RESOURCES

To learn more about the Shoshone, please visit **abdobooklinks.com** or scan this QR code. These links are routinely monitored and updated to provide the most current information available.

Index

bands 6, 16, 24
Bear River 24
Bighorn Mountains 4

California 4, 28
ceremonies 6, 10, 18, 28
chiefs 6, 26
children 16, 18
clothing 12, 14, 16
crafts 14, 18, 28

diseases 24

elders 16, 18, 28
Europeans 22, 24

family 6, 10, 16
federal recognition 28
fishing 6, 10, 16
food 8, 10, 28

games 18
gathering 6, 10, 18
Green River 4

homelands 4, 22, 24
homes 8
hunting 6, 10, 16, 22, 24

Idaho 4, 28

language 4, 28
Lewis and Clark 24

medicine people 6
Montana 4

Nevada 4, 28

Pacific Ocean 24

reservations 28

Sacagawea 24
Snake River 4
spiritual leader 6
stories 14, 18, 20, 28

tools 8, 10, 14, 16, 18, 22, 26

Uinta Mountains 4
Utah 4, 28

war 6, 22, 24, 26
war leader 6
Washakie 26
weapons 22
Wyoming 4, 28